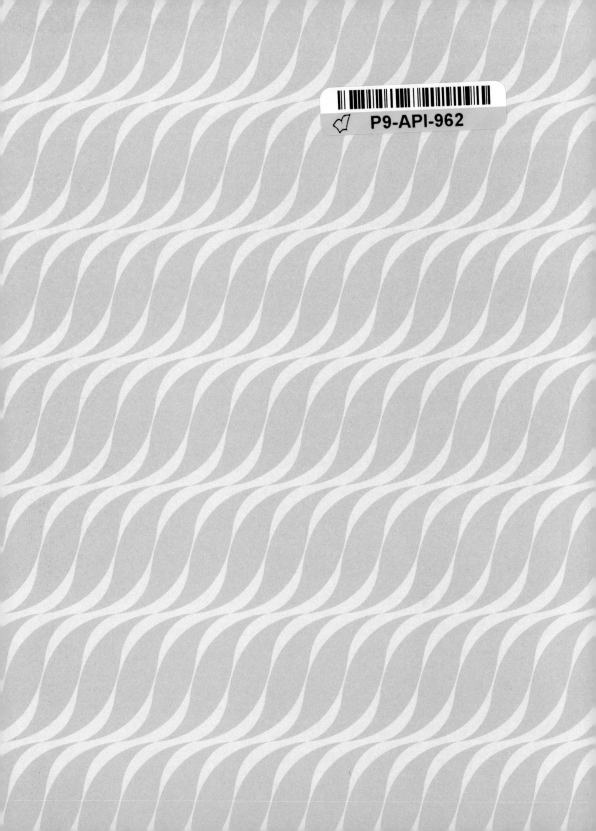

the hunt for food

michael chinery

southwater

This edition is published by Southwater

Southwater is an imprint of Anness Publishing Ltd
Hermes House, 88–89 Blackfriars Road, London SE1 8HA
tel. 020 7401 2077; fax 020 7633 9499
www.southwaterbooks.com; info@anness.com

UK agent: The Manning Partnership Ltd, 6 The Old Dairy, Melcombe Road, Bath BA2 3LR;
tel. 01225 478444; fax 01225 478440; sales@manning-partnership.co.uk

UK distributor: Grantham Book Services Ltd, Isaac Newton Way, Alma Park Industrial Estate, Grantham,
Lincs NG31 9SD; tel. 01476 541080; fax 01476 541061; orders@gbs.tbs-ltd.co.uk

North American agent/distributor: National Book Network, 4501 Forbes Boulevard,
Suite 200, Lanham, MD 20706; tel. 301 459 3366; fax 301 429 5746; www.nbnbooks.com

Australian agent/distributor: Pan Macmillan Australia, Level 18, St Martins Tower, 31 Market St,
Sydney, NSW 2000; tel. 1300 135 113; fax 1300 135 103; customer.service@macmillan.com.au

New Zealand agent/distributor: David Bateman Ltd, 30 Tarndale Grove, Off Bush Road, Albany, Auckland;
tel. (09) 415 7664; fax (09) 415 8892

Publisher: Joanna Lorenz
Managing Editor: Linda Fraser
Editors: Sarah Uttridge, Rebecca Clunes
Editorial Consultant: Gilly Cameron Cooper
Editorial Reader: Jonathan Marshall
Authors: Michael Bright, John Farndon, Robin Kerrod, Rhonda Klevansky, Dr Jen Green, Barbara Taylor
Illustrators:, Julian Baker, Peter Bull, Vanessa Card, Stuart Carter, Linden Artists, Rob Sheffield Sarah
Smith, David Webb

Previously published as *Wild Animal Planet: The Hunt for Food*

10 9 8 7 6 5 4 3 2

ABPL: Nigel Dennis: 46t /Paul Funston: 37cl /Dave Hamman: 43tr / Clem Haagner: 44t /Beverly Joubert: 42c /Peter Lillie: 42b, 47t /Anup Shah: 46c.
Heather Angel: 29bl. E.T Archive: 38tr. BBC Natural History Unit: Bruce Davidson: 55tl /Lockwood and Dattari: 51br/Jeff Foott: 41tl /Tony Heald: 27tr/Hans
Kristophe Kappel: 41br /J Rotman: 61tl /Image select: 37br /Keith Scholey: 47b/A Shah 25t /Vadim Sidorovich: 48t. Biophotos: Adam Britton: 23cl.
Bridgeman Art Library: 42t, 50t. Bruce Coleman: 18tl, 19cr, 34bl, 57tl, 58t, 59t /Ingo Arndt: 54tl./J Brackenbury: 13bl /Erwin and Peggy Bauer: 38br, 44bl,
45b /Bruce Davidson: 52t, 52b, 53cl/Christer Fredriksson: 43b /Sir J Grayson: 11tl /Leonard Lee Rue: 45c /Antonio Manzanares: 28tr, 43tl/ Joe Mcdonald:
45t /Jon Taylor: 14t /Kim Taylor: 11br, 16bl /Gunter Ziesler: 44br. Mary Evans Picture Library: 11cl, 29tr. FLPA: 18bl, 57cl, 57cr /F Polking: 12tr, 46b, 47c
/Larry West: 15b/Martin Withers: 36b. Gallo Images: Clem Haagner: 29m /Eric Reisinger: 29tl. Garden Wildlife Matters: M Collins: 13br. Images Colour
Library: 30 – 31. Innerspace Visions: B Cropp: 61cl, S Drogin: 60tl, M S Nolan: 61bl /M Synderman: 60br. Natural Science Photos: 56c. NHPA: 7tr, 7bl, 8t,
9tl, 9br, 15tr, 18br, 19tl/Daryl Balfour: 36cl /K Ghani: 49t /D Heuchlin: 23t. T Kitchin & V Hurst: 51br /Kevin Schaffer: 40bl. Only Horses: 35br. Oxford
Scientific Films: 6r, 7br, 9tr, 9bl, 20-21, 56tl, 58b, 59b /Anthony Bannister: 49cr /G I Bernard: 27br /David Cayless: 53t, 53cr, 53b /Martyn Colbeck:37tr
/Daniel J Cox: 39bl /Richard Day: 48b /M Deeble and V Stone: 22tl /David C Fritts: 40tr, 41bl / Mark Hamblin: 27tl /Dave Hamman: 33bl /Mike Hill: 59tr
/Lon E Lauber: 51bl /Martin Leach: 49cl /Stan Osolinski: 26b, 36tr /Nikita Ovsyanikov: 39tr
/Andrew Plumptre: 55br /Michael Sewell: 49b /Nivek Sinha: 39br /G Soury: 61br /David
Tipling: 35bl /Tom Walker: 39tl, 40tr/Konrad Wothe: 28bl. Planet Earth: 33tl, 56b,
57b /G Bell: 23c /G du Feu:10br /N Greaves: 24tl. S Hopkin: 10bl /B
Kenney: 11cr / D Maitland: 15tl /J Scott: 24bl, 25b /A and M Shah:
25c /Anup Shah: 54br, 55cl. Paplilio: Kim Taylor: 26tl, 30tl, 30tr,
31m, 31tl. Premaphotos Wildlife: 16t, 16br, 17b /K Preston-
Mafham: 13cr /Kim Taylor: 10tl. Kim Taylor: 6l. Warren
Photographic: 8b, /Kim Taylor: 12bl, 12cr, 17t. 27bl.

Contents

The Diet of Animals

All living things need food of some kind or another. Food provides them with the energy needed to move about and to power all of life's other activities. Food also provides the "building blocks" needed for growth. Plants use the energy in sunlight to make their own food by a process called photosynthesis, but animals all have to find and eat "ready-made" food in the form of plants or other animals. Animals that feed on plants are called herbivores. Those that eat meat or flesh are called carnivores and those that regularly eat both plants and other animals are called omnivores. We are omnivores, and so are chimpanzees and most bears.

Pandas have given up regular hunting in favour of a diet of bamboo.

Sensing food

Herbivorous animals generally track down tasty foods by using their eyes and sense of smell. Nectar-seeking butterflies, for example, home in on flowers by picking up their colors and scents, and grazing mammals can smell fresh grass from many miles away. Carnivores use their eyes, their sense of smell and also their ears to find food. Many snakes track down their prey by flicking out their tongues to pick up traces of scent on the ground or in the air. Rattlesnakes have heat-sensitive pits on their snouts that tell them when warm-blooded prey is near. This is particularly useful at night. Hearing is also important for animals that hunt at night. Owls have excellent hearing as well as superb eyesight. Their ears pick up the slightest rustle in the grass below and enable the owls to home in on their prey with amazing accuracy. Soft-edged feathers enable the owls to fly very quietly, so the prey does not hear them coming.

Snakes use their senses to detect other animals and, instead of hunting, many snakes simply lie in wait for their prey to come to them.

4

To chase or to lie in wait?

Meat-eaters have two main ways of getting their food. They can chase after their prey, or they can hide and lie in wait for it. Wolves and other dogs are chasers, often hunting in packs to catch prey much larger than themselves. The chase can last for hours, with the dogs taking turns at the front. Lions and other cats also chase their prey, but their chases are much shorter. Leopards sometimes lie in wait for their prey, often sitting on a branch or a rock and dropping on anything that passes beneath. Some crab spiders lurk in flowers and often blend so well with the petals that they are very hard to see. Insects visiting the flowers for a drink are quickly grabbed by the spiders. Many spiders make sticky webs to trap their prey but some rely on sensing the vibrations when prey walk over or near their webs.

Most big cats are only too happy to eat someone else's meal and steal kills from other animals whenever they can. Cheetahs are an exception, and eat only animals they have killed themselves.

Teeth and claws

Most predators use their claws or teeth to catch and kill their prey. Cats, for example, use their powerful claws to bring down their victims, and then kill them either by biting through the neck or by gripping the throat until their prey suffocates. Birds of prey usually use their talons to snatch and kill their victims. The birds then use their hooked beaks to tear up the flesh, although owls usually swallow their prey whole. Mammalian teeth vary with the animals' diets. Grass-eaters have big grinding teeth to crush grass and release as much of the goodness from it as possible. Meat-eaters have sharp-edged cheek teeth for slicing through the flesh of their prey. Insect jaws are on the outside of the body and they cut or crush the food before pushing it into their mouth. Bugs feed on liquids by piercing plants or other animals with sharp, tubular beaks. Butterflies suck up nectar with slender "drinking straws."

Eagles attack with their talons. They are so long, sharp and deeply curved that one swipe is usually enough to kill their prey.

All depend on plants

Whatever they eat, all animals depend on plants for their food. Lions eat zebras and antelopes but the nutrition provided by the meat of these grazing animals comes from their diet of grass and other plants. Even sharks depend on plants as the fish that they eat feed on plants floating near the surface of the sea.

A swallowtail butterfly using its long tongue to suck up nectar.

Insect Plant-eaters

Many insect species are herbivores (plant-eaters), including caterpillars, most bugs and some beetles. Different insects specialize in eating particular parts of plants – the leaves, buds, seeds, roots or bark. Many plant-eating insects become pests when they feed on cultivated plants or crops. Other pests nibble things that humans would not consider edible, such as clothes, carpets and wooden furniture.

Beetles and bugs do not always eat the same food throughout their lives. Rose chafer beetles, for example, nibble petals and pollen, but their larvae (young) feed on rotting wood. Some adult beetles and bugs do not feed at all. Instead, they put all their energy into finding a mate and reproducing.

▲ TUNNEL-BORERS
Female bark beetles lay their eggs under the tree's bark. When the young hatch, each one eats its way through the soft wood just under the bark, creating a long, narrow tunnel just wide enough to squeeze through.

Did you know?
Wood boring beetle grubs may eat for 7 years before they reach full size.

squash bug
(Coreus marginatus)

◄ SQUASH-LOVERS
Squash bugs are named after their favourite food. The squash-plant family includes courgettes and pumpkins. This bug is about to pierce a courgette flower bud and suck out its sap. Most squash bugs are green or brown. They feed on leaves, flowers and seeds. The insects are serious pests in North America.

▲ A PLAGUE OF APHIDS

Aphids are small, soft-bodied bugs. They use their sharp, beak-like mouths to pierce plant leaves and stems and suck out the life-giving sap that is found inside. Aphids reproduce so quickly in warm weather that they can cover a plant within a few hours – and suck it dry.

▲ BEETLE ATTACK

Colorado beetles are high on the list of dangerous insects in many countries. The beetles originally came from the western USA, where they ate the leaves of local plants. When European settlers came and cultivated potatoes, the beetles ate the crop and did great damage. Colorado beetles later spread to become a major pest in Europe, but are now controlled by pesticides.

▲ SCALY FEEDERS

Most female scale insects have neither legs nor wings, but they can be identified as bugs as they have sucking mouthparts (beetles have biting jaws). Scale insects are usually hidden under waxy or horny scales, as shown here. The insects are piercing the skin of a juicy melon and sucking its juices.

▲ THE EVIL WEEVIL

These grains of wheat have been infested by a type of beetle called the grain weevil. The adult weevils bore through the grain's hard case with their long snouts to reach the soft kernel inside. Females lay their eggs inside the kernels. Then, when the young hatch, they can feed in safety.

Beetle and Bug Attack

ground beetle
(Loricera pilicornis)

▲ **SPEEDY HUNTER**

A ground beetle feeds on a juicy worm it has caught. Ground beetles are a large family of over 20,000 species. Many species cannot fly, hence their name. However, most ground beetles are fast runners. The beetle uses its speed to overtake a fleeing victim. Once trapped, the victim is firmly grabbed in the attacker's powerful jaws.

Some insects eat only vegetable matter, others are carnivores (meat-eaters). Some of the carnivorous species hunt and kill live prey, while others are scavengers and feed on dead animals. There are also parasitic insects that live on larger animals and eat their flesh or suck their blood, without killing them. Most insect predators feed on insects of around their own size. Some, however, tackle larger game, such as frogs, fish, tadpoles, snails and worms. Insects are adapted in different ways to catch and overpower their prey.

All beetles have jaws, which are used by the carnivorous species to seize and crush or crunch up their victims. Bugs have jointed mouthparts made for sucking living victims' juices from their bodies.

◄ **GONE FISHING**

Great diving beetles are fierce aquatic hunters. They hunt fish, tadpoles, newts and minibeasts that live in ponds and streams. This beetle has caught a stickleback. It grabs the fish in its jaws, then injects it with digestive juices that begin to dissolve the fish's flesh. When the victim finally stops struggling and dies, the beetle begins to feed.

Famous Victim

Charles Darwin (1809–1882), the British naturalist who first developed the theory of evolution, is thought by some to have been bitten by a South American assassin bug. Darwin had gone to South America to study wildlife. On his return to Britain, he fell victim to a mysterious illness, which weakened him for the rest of his life. Some historians believe that when the assassin bug bit into Darwin for a blood snack, it transmitted a dangerous disease.

▲ VAMPIRE BEETLE

The person on which this assassin bug has landed will not feel a thing, as the bug has injected a pain killer. These bugs are found world wide, especially in the tropics. Most of them hunt minibeasts and suck their juices dry.

shield bug

EATEN ALIVE ▶

Although most shield bugs are plant-eaters, this one is not. Some species start their lives as herbivores and move on to a mixed diet later. This one has caught a caterpillar, and uses its curving mouthparts to suck its prey dry. The bugs use their front legs to hold their victims steady while they feast on them.

Did you know? Bedbugs check the smell and temperature of hosts before feeding on them.

◀ NO ESCAPE

When attacked, snails withdraw into their shells and seal them with slime, but this is no defence against a snail-hunting beetle, which squirts liquid into the shell to dissolve the slime and kill the snail. The snail-hunters usually have narrow heads that they can push right inside the shells.

Hungry Caterpillars

Caterpillars are streamlined eating machines. They must store enough energy to turn into adult moths or butterflies. Their bodies are like expandable sacks, fitted with strong mandibles (jaws) that are edged with teeth or blunt grinding plates. Caterpillars munch through several times their own body weight of food in a single day, and grow incredibly fast.

A caterpillar's first meal is usually the eggshell from which it has hatched. It then moves on to the next food source. Some species eat unhatched eggs or even other caterpillars. Most feed on the leaves and stems of a particular food plant – which is usually the one on which they hatched. The caterpillar stage lasts for at least two weeks, and sometimes much longer.

tunnel left by leaf-mining caterpillar

▲ LEAF MINING
Many tiny caterpillars eat their way through the inside of a leaf instead of crawling across the surface. This activity is known as leaf mining. Often, their progress is revealed by a pale tunnel beneath the leaf surface.

sensitive palps are located near the mouth

legs are used to grip leaves while eating

swallowtail butterfly caterpillar
(Papilio machaon)

▲ FEEDING HABITS
Caterpillars eat different food plants from those visited by adult insects. Swallowtail butterfly caterpillars feed on fennel, carrots and milk-parsley. The adult butterflies drink the nectar of many different flowers.

IDENTIFYING FOOD ▶
The head end of a privet hawk moth caterpillar is shown in close-up here. A caterpillar probably identifies food using sensitive organs called palps, which are just in front of the mouth.

◄ FAST EATERS

Cabbages are the main food of the caterpillars of the large white butterfly. These insects can strip a field of leaves in a few nights. Many farmers and gardeners kill caterpillars with pesticides. The caterpillar population may also be kept down by parasitic wasps that attack the caterpillars.

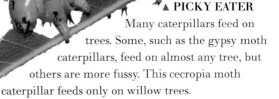

▲ PICKY EATER

Many caterpillars feed on trees. Some, such as the gypsy moth caterpillars, feed on almost any tree, but others are more fussy. This cecropia moth caterpillar feeds only on willow trees.

Alice in Wonderland

In Lewis Carroll's story Alice in Wonderland, *a pipe-smoking caterpillar discusses with Alice what it is like to change size. Carroll was probably thinking of how fast caterpillars grow as a result of their non-stop eating.*

▲ PROCESSIONARY CATERPILLARS

The caterpillars of processionary moths rest together in silken nests, and travel to their feeding areas in long lines. These insects are poisonous and do not hide from predators.

Butterfly Food

postman butterfly
(*Heliconius*)

Many flowers produce a sugary fluid called nectar. This attracts insects in search of a meal, including butterflies and bees. Butterflies and moths do not have jaws and teeth, as they did in the caterpillar stage of their development. Instead, they suck up fluids through long, tubular proboscises, which act like drinking straws. Most butterflies survive exclusively on nectar. They spend most of their brief lives flitting from flower to flower in search of this juice. Some woodland species extract sweet liquids from other sources, such as rotting fruit and sap oozing from wounds in trees. A few species even suck on dung. Butterflies rarely live for more than a few days, as none of their foods is very nutritious.

▲ POISONOUS PLANTS
The larvae of *Heliconius* butterflies feed on passion flowers in the rain forests of South America. They absorb the plant's poison. It does not hurt them, but makes them unpalatable to birds. The adult butterflies also feed on the plant. They can detoxify the poison.

red admiral butterfly
(*Vanessa atalanta*)

▼ CIDER DRINKING
In autumn, butterflies such as the red admiral and the Camberwell beauty often feed on rotting fruit. Sometimes the juice has fermented to alcohol, and the red admiral may be seen reeling around as if drunk.

▲ FRUIT EATERS
The first generation of comma butterflies appears each year in early summer. These insects feed on the delicate white blossoms of blackberries, because the fruit has not ripened at this time. The second generation appears in autumn, and feeds on the ripe blackberry fruits.

◄ DRINKING STRAW

Many flowers have nectaries inside the blooms to draw insects on to their pollen sacs. The insects carry pollen on to other flowers as they feed, and pollinate them. Some butterflies have very long proboscises to reach deep stores of nectar.

Did you know? The purple emperor butterfly often survives by sucking juices from the rotting bodies of dead animals.

▲ HOVERING HAWK MOTHS

The day-flying hummingbird hawk moth gets its name from its habit of hovering in front of flowers like a hummingbird. It sips nectar from this mid-flight position, rather than landing on the flower. Hawk moths have the longest proboscises of all butterflies and moths. The proboscis of the Darwin's hawk moth is 30–35cm long, which is about three times the length of its body.

► WOODLAND VARIETY

Many woodland butterflies extract juices from a variety of sources. The speckled wood butterfly sometimes sips nectar from bluebells. However, it feeds mainly on honeydew, the sugary secretion of tiny insects called aphids. The leaves of plants are often coated with honeydew.

▲ NIGHT FEEDER

Noctuid moths often sip nectar from ragworts in meadows by moonlight. In temperate countries, these moths mostly feed on warm summer nights. They get their name from the Latin word *noctuis*, which means night.

speckled wood
butterfly
(*Pararge aegeria*)

13

Spider Traps

Many spiders catch their prey on a sticky web, but this is only one of many quite different ways of catching or trapping food. Some spiders lurk inside hidden tubes of silk or underground burrows and wait patiently. Silk threads around the entrance trip up passing insects and other small creatures. Inside the burrow, the spider feels the tug on its trip lines, giving it time to rush out and pounce on the prey before it can escape. Lie-in-wait spiders include trapdoor spiders, which have special spines on their fangs to rake away the soil as they dig their burrows.

▲ SILK DOORS
The lid of a trapdoor spider's burrow is made of silk and soil. The door fits tightly into the burrow opening and may be camouflaged with twigs and leaves. In areas liable to flooding, walls or turrets are built around the entrance to keep out the water.

▲ A SILKEN TUBE
This purse-web spider has emerged from its burrow. It usually lies in wait for prey inside its tubular purse of densely woven silk. The tube is about 45cm long and about the thickness of a finger. Part of it sticks out of the ground or from a tree trunk, and is well camouflaged with debris.

a purse-web spider waits for an insect to land on its tube-like web

an insect is speared by the spider's sharp jaws

▲ INSIDE A PURSE-WEB
The spider waits inside its silken purse for an insect to walk over the tube. It spears the insect through the tube with its sharp jaws and drags the prey inside.

▲ FUNNEL-WEB SPIDERS

The Sydney funnel-web is one of the deadliest spiders in the world. It lives in an underground burrow lined with silk. Leading from the mouth of the burrow is a funnel that can be up to 1m across. Trip wires are also strung from the funnel, so that when an insect hits one, the spider is alerted. The spider can dig its own burrow with its fangs, but prefers to use existing holes and cracks. Funnel-web spiders eat beetles, snails and other small animals.

▲ TRIP WIRES

The giant trapdoor spider may place silken trip lines around the entrance to its burrow to detect the movements of a passing meal. If it does not have trip lines, the spider relies on feeling the vibrations of prey through the ground. If it senses a meal is nearby, it rushes from the burrow to grab the prey in its jaws.

Did you know? Trapdoor spiders may live up to 20 years in their burrows.

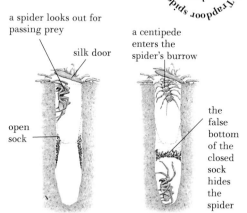

a spider looks out for passing prey

silk door

a centipede enters the spider's burrow

open sock

the false bottom of the closed sock hides the spider

▲ ODD SPIDER OUT

A tiger wolf spider has dug out soil with its fangs and lined the walls of its burrow with silk. Most wolf spiders do not burrow. Instead, they chase their food, using their sharp vision and fangs to capture live insect prey.

▲ ALL KINDS OF TRAPS

Trapdoor spider burrows range from simple tubes to elaborate lairs with hidden doors and escape tunnels. The burrow of *Anidiops villosus* has a collapsible sock. The spider pulls it down to form a false bottom, hiding it from predators.

The Hunt of the

The salticid jumping spiders are a huge spider family of about 5,000 species. They are found all over the world, and most are squat, hairy and dull in color, although some tropical species have splashes of brilliant, iridescent color. All jumping spiders, however, have big, bulging eyes—all the better to hunt with! (If a human looks at a jumping spider, it will turn its tiny head to peer back.) As a family, salticids have the sharpest eyesight of any spider. Most species are constantly darting along jerkily, on the lookout for prey. They see in color and form clear images of their victims, stalking as a cat stalks a mouse, crouching before the final pounce.

SIGN LANGUAGE
A male jumping spider's front legs are longer and thicker than a female's. He waves them about in courtship dances, like a sign language.

PREPARATION
Before it takes off, a jumping spider anchors itself firmly to a surface with a silk safety line. It pushes off with its four back legs and leaps on to the target. The Australian flying spider has wing-like flaps that enable it to glide through the air.

STURDY LEGS
This female heavy jumper is feeding on a leaf hopper. A jumping spider's legs do not seem to be specially adapted for jumping. Their small size (less than ¾ inch long) and light weight probably help them to make amazing leaps.

Jumping Spider

THE BIG LEAP

A jumping spider's strong front legs are often raised before a jump. They stretch forward in the air, and grip fast on the prey when the spider lands. Hairy tufts on the feet help jumping spiders to grip surfaces that are smooth and vertical. They can even leap away from a vertical surface to seize a flying insect.

JUMPING CANNIBALS

This female two-striped jumping spider is feeding on another member of the salticid family. Some *Portia* jumping spiders vibrate the webs of orb-weaving spiders, imitating the movement of an insect struggling to escape. When the orb-weaver comes to investigate, the *Portia* spider pounces on it.

A Snake's Rare Meal

Snakes are all predators, but different species eat different foods and hunt in different ways. Some snakes eat a wide variety of prey, while others have a more specialized diet. Snakes have to make the most of each meal because they move fairly slowly and may not catch prey very often. A snake's body works at a slow rate, which means that it can go for months without eating.

▲ TREE HUNTERS
A rat snake, from North America, grasps a baby bluebird in its jaws and begins the process of digestion. Rat snakes often slither up trees in search of baby birds, eggs or squirrels.

rat snake
(Elaphe)

▲ FISHY SNACKS
The tentacled snake of southern Asia lives on fish. It hides among plants in the water and ambushes passing prey.

▼ TRICKY LURE
The Australasian death adder's colorful tail tip looks like a worm. The adder wriggles the "worm" to lure birds and small mammals.

◄ EGG-EATERS
The African egg-eater snake checks an egg with its tongue to make sure it is fresh. Then it swallows the egg whole. It uses the pointed ends of the bones in its backbone to crack the eggshell. It eats the egg and then coughs up the crushed shell.

SURPRISE ATTACK ►
Lunch for this gaboon viper is a mouse. The viper hides among dry leaves on the forest floors of West and Central Africa. Its coloring and markings camouflage it well. It waits for a small animal to pass, then grabs hold of it in a surprise attack. Many other snakes that hunt by day also ambush their prey.

Did you know? Sometimes a snake coughs up its prey alive!

smooth snake
(Coronella austriaca)

◄ SNAKE SNACK
This smooth snake is eating an asp viper. The viper fits neatly inside the body of the smooth snake. This makes it easier to swallow than animals that are a different shape.

A Rat Snake's Lunch

1 Rat snakes feed on rats, mice, voles, lizards, birds and eggs. Many of them hunt at night. They are good climbers and can even go up tree trunks with smooth bark and no branches. The snakes find their prey by following a scent trail or waiting to ambush an animal.

Rat snakes are members of the world's largest snake family. They have more flexible skulls than more primitive snakes, such as pythons and boas, and their lower jaw is split into two unconnected halves. These adaptations enable the snakes to open their mouths very wide and to swallow their prey whole. The rat snake's favorite food are rodents such as voles and rats.

2 When the rat snake is near enough to its prey, it strikes quickly. Its sharp teeth sink into the victim's body to stop it running or flying away. The snake then loops its coils around the victim as fast as possible, before the animal can bite or scratch to defend itself.

3 Each time the vole breathes out, the rat snake squeezes around the victim's rib cage to stop it breathing in again. Breathing becomes impossible, and the victim soon dies from suffocation.

20

4 Once the victim is dead, the rat snake loosens its coils and begins the process of swallowing. It unhinges its jaws and "walks" its mouth over its meal. The loose lower jaw stretches sideways to fit around the shape of the dead prey.

5 The rat snake swallows its meal head first. As the vole moves down the snake's throat, its legs fold back against the sides of its body. The way the fur lies makes it easier to swallow the vole The snake's skin stretches as the meal moves down its body.

6 As the vole moves farther down inside the snake's body, the skin stretches more. The ribs move apart at the front to make space for the vole's body. The snake pushes its windpipe to the front of its mouth, so that it can use it like a snorkel for breathing. It may take only one or two gulps for a snake to swallow a small animal whole.

Crocodile Snacks

A big crocodile can survive for up to two years between meals. It lives off fat stored in its tail and other parts of its body. Generally, though, crocodilians (crocodiles, alligators and caimans) eat a lot of fish, although their strong jaws may snap up anything that wanders too close. Young crocodilians eat small animals such as insects, snails and frogs, while adults feed on birds, turtles and mammals. Big Nile crocodiles tackle large animals such as zebras and wildebeest when they visit the rivers to drink. Crocodiles cannot chew and have to tear large prey apart before swallowing it. They eat small prey whole, bones and all. Crocodiles also scavenge on dead animals.

Most crocodilians hunt at night and save energy by sitting and waiting for their food to pass their way. They may stalk prey, lunging forward or leaping out of the water to capture it. In water, a crocodile may sweep its open jaws from side to side to catch its next meal.

▲ SURPRISE ATTACK
A Nile crocodile lunges from the water at an incredible speed to grab a wildebeest in its powerful jaws. It is difficult for the wildebeest to jump back as the river bank slopes steeply into the water. The crocodile will plunge back into the water, dragging its prey with it in order to drown it.

▼ CHEEKY BIRDS
Large crocodiles feed on wading birds such as this saddlebill stork. Birds, however, often seem to know when they are in no danger from a crocodile. Plovers have been seen standing on the gums of crocodiles and even pecking at the fearsome teeth for leftovers. A marabou stork was once seen stealing a fish right out of a crocodile's mouth.

SMALLER PREY

This dwarf caiman, hiding in floating debris, has just snapped up a tasty bullfrog. Caimans and other small crocodilians eat lots of frogs and toads, and also catch fish. The slim, pointed teeth of the Indian gharial are ideal for grasping any slippery fish that is within range, but its jaws are not strong enough to tackle anything bigger.

◄ SWALLOWING PREY

A crocodile raises its head and grips a crab firmly at the back of its throat. After several jerky head movements the crab is correctly positioned to be eaten whole. High levels of acid in the crocodile's stomach help it break down the crab's hard shell so that every part is digested.

Did you know? A Nile crocodile has a stomach that is about the size of a basketball.

FISHY FOOD

A Nile crocodile swallows a fish head first so that the fish's spines do not stick in its throat. Fish make up about 70 per cent of the diet of most crocodilians, especially the narrow snouted species, such as the gharial of northern India and the African slender-snouted crocodile. The narrowness of the snout offers little water resistance in the sideways sweeping movement used to catch fish.

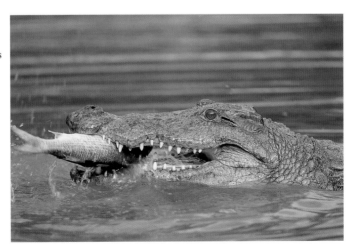

Ambush on

1 A Nile crocodile is nearly invisible as it lies almost submerged in wait for its prey. Only eyes, ears and nostrils are showing. The crocodile lurks in places where it knows prey will regularly visit the river. The dark olive of its skin is well camouflaged against the murky water. It may disappear completely beneath the water. Some crocodilians can hold their breath for more than an hour while they are submerged.

A crocodile quietly drifting near the shore looks just like a harmless, floating log. This is just a disguise as it waits for an unsuspecting animal to come down to the river to drink. The crocodile is in luck. A herd of zebras come to cross the river. The crocodile launches its attack with astonishing speed. Shooting forwards, it snaps shut its powerful jaws and sharp teeth like a vice around a zebra's leg or muzzle. The stunned zebra is pulled into deeper water to be drowned. Other crocodiles are attracted to the large kill. They gather round to bite into the carcass, rotating in the water to twist off large chunks of flesh. Grazing animals constantly risk death-by-crocodile to drink or cross water. There is little they can do to defend themselves from the attack of such a large predator.

2 The crocodile erupts from the water, taking the zebras by surprise. It lunges at its victim with a fast burst of energy. The crocodile must overcome its prey quickly as it cannot chase a zebra overland. It is also easily exhausted and takes a long time to recover from exercise of any kind.

the River Nile

3 The crocodile seizes, pulls and shakes the zebra in its powerful jaws. The victim's neck is sometimes broken in the attack and it dies quickly. More often the shocked animal is dragged into the water, struggling feebly against its attacker.

4 The crocodile drags the zebra into deeper water and holds it down to drown it. It may also spin round in a roll, until the prey stops breathing. The crocodile twists or rolls around over and over again, with the animal clamped in its jaws, until the prey is dead.

5 A freshly killed zebra attracts Nile crocodiles from all around. A large kill is too difficult for one crocodile to defend on its own. Several crocodiles take it in turns to share the feast and may help each other to tear the carcass apart. They fasten their jaws on to a part of the body and turn over and over in the water until a chunk of meat is twisted loose and can be swallowed whole.

A Swift Attack from Above

sparrow hawk
(Accipiter nisus)

Birds of prey hunt in different ways. A raptor, which is another name for any bird of prey, may sit on a perch and simply wait for a meal to appear on the ground or fly past. This technique is called "still-hunting." Other birds search for prey by flying low over open ground, or darting in and out of cover such as a clump of trees. Kestrels are among the raptors that hover in the air while looking for prey, and then swoop down suddenly on it. Peregrine falcons are noted for their spectacular dives, or stoops. With wings almost folded, they dive on their prey from a great height, accelerating up to perhaps 185 miles per hour. Their aim is to strike the prey at high speed to kill it instantly. Peregrines either snatch prey from the air, or pick it off the ground.

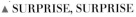

▲ SURPRISE, SURPRISE
The sparrow hawk uses surprise and speed to make a kill. It flies under cover until it spots a potential meal, then dashes out into the open to snatch its unsuspecting prey at speed.

◄ PLUCKY EAGLE
An American bald eagle plucks a cattle egret it has just killed. The bird makes a change from the eagle's usual diet of fish. Most birds of prey pluck the feathers from birds they have caught before eating, as they cannot digest them. Owls are the only raptors to swallow their prey whole.

bald eagle
(Haliaeetus leucocephalus)

buzzard
(Buteo buteo)

◀ RABBIT RELISH

A common buzzard stands guard over the rabbit it has just killed. Over grassland, the buzzard hunts on the wing, sometimes hovering like a kestrel. Where there are trees or rocks, it may perch on a high point until it sights prey. The buzzard then swoops in for the kill.

▲ IN HOT PURSUIT

An African harrier hawk chases doves along the river bank. Such chases more often than not end in failure. This hawk is about the same size as a typical harrier, but it has longer wings.

▼ IT'S A COVER-UP

A kestrel spreads its wings in an attempt to cover up the mouse it is preparing to eat on its feeding post. This behavior is known as mantling, and is common among birds of prey. They do it to hide their food from other hungry birds that may try to rob them.

▼ MAKING A MEAL OF IT

A kestrel tucks into its kill on its favorite feeding post. The bird holds the prey with its feet and tears the flesh into small pieces with its sharp bill. It swallows small bones, but often discards big ones. Later, as with most raptors, it regurgitates pellets containing fur and other indigestible parts of its prey.

kestrel
(Falco tinnunculus)

Raptor Food

Birds of prey hunt all kinds of animals. Many attack other birds, such as sparrows, starlings and pigeons, which are usually taken in the air. Some raptors hunt small mammals, such as rabbits, rats, mice and voles. Large species of eagle may tackle even larger mammals. The Philippine eagle, and the harpy eagle of South America, for example, pluck monkeys from the rainforest canopy. Both species are massive birds, with bodies 3 feet long. Serpent eagles and secretary birds feast on snakes and other reptiles. Small birds of prey often feed on insects and worms. Most species will also supplement their diet by scavenging on carrion (the meat of dead animals) whenever they find it.

▲ INSECT INSIDE

A lesser kestrel prepares to eat a grasshopper it has just caught on a rooftop in Spain. This kestrel lives mainly on insects. It catches grasshoppers and beetles on the ground, and all kinds of flying insects while on the wing. When there are plenty of insects, flocks of lesser kestrels feed together. Unlike the larger common kestrel, the lesser kestrel does not hover when hunting.

golden eagle
(*Aquila chrysaetos*)

◄ GOLDEN HUNTER

A golden eagle stands guard over the squirrel it has just caught. This eagle usually hunts at low levels. It flushes out prey—mainly rabbits, hares and grouse—which it catches and kills on the ground. Whenever they get the chance, golden eagles also eat carrion.

martial eagle
(Polemaetus bellicosus)

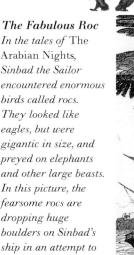

The Fabulous Roc
In the tales of The Arabian Nights, *Sinbad the Sailor encountered enormous birds called rocs. They looked like eagles, but were gigantic in size, and preyed on elephants and other large beasts. In this picture, the fearsome rocs are dropping huge boulders on Sinbad's ship in an attempt to finally destroy him.*

▲ REPTILIAN SNACK

A martial eagle stands over its lizard kill in the Kruger National Park, South Africa. This is Africa's biggest eagle, and it is capable of taking prey as big as a small antelope.

Did you know? 12 species of birds of prey eat only insects

▼ SNAIL SPECIALIST

A snail kite eyes its next meal. This is the most specialized feeder among birds of prey, eating only freshwater snails. It breeds in the Everglades National Park, Florida.

▲ COBRA KILLER

A pale chanting goshawk has caught and killed a yellow cobra. The chanting goshawks earned their name because of their noisy calls in the breeding season. The African plains are the hunting grounds of both the pale and the dark chanting goshawks, which feed mainly on lizards and snakes but also eat small mammals.

snail kite
(Rostrhamus sociabilis)

29

The Barn Owl's

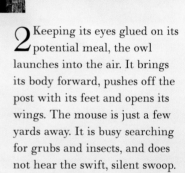

1 An owl waits for a rustle in the undergrowth. Suddenly it hears something. It swivels its head, and its sensitive ears pinpoint exactly where the sound is coming from. The owl then spots its prey—a mouse rummaging among the leaf litter on the ground.

2 Keeping its eyes glued on its potential meal, the owl launches into the air. It brings its body forward, pushes off the post with its feet and opens its wings. The mouse is just a few yards away. It is busy searching for grubs and insects, and does not hear the swift, silent swoop.

The barn owl is found on all continents except Antarctica. It is easily recognizable because of its white, heart-shaped facial disc. Its eyes are relatively small for an owl, but it can still see well at night. The barn owl tracks its prey as much by ear as by eye. Its hearing is particularly keen, because the feathers on its facial disc channel sounds into its ears with great precision. The owl featured here is "still-hunting"—the tactic of watching for prey from a favorite perch. However, barn owls also often hunt on the wing. They cruise slowly and silently back and forth over their feeding grounds until they hear or spy prey, then swoop down silently for the kill.

Silent Strike

3 The owl makes a beeline for its prey with powerful beats of its wings. Even though it is travelling quite fast, it still makes no sound. Dense, soft feathers cover its wings and legs and muffle the sound of air flowing over them. Its noiseless flight allows the owl to concentrate on the sounds that the mouse is making and so keep track of its prey.

5 Now only a few inches above the ground, the owl thrusts its feet forward, claws spread wide, and drops on the prey. At the same time, it spreads its wings and tail to slow down the approach. The hunter's aim is deadly. Its talons close round the mouse and crush it to death. Then the owl transfers the dead mouse to its beak and returns to its perch. The owl will swallow the mouse head first.

4 The mouse at last begins to sense that something is wrong. For an instant it is glued to the spot in fear. Then it starts to run for its life. However, the owl is more than a match for it. By making use of its rounded wings and broad tail, the bird can twist and turn easily in the air, following the scuttling mouse at every change of direction.

Eating on the Hoof

The world's most successful herbivores (plant-eaters) are animals with hoofs, such as horses, cattle, deer and sheep. They use speed, endurance and sure-footedness to escape predators, and have digestive systems that make the most of vegetable diets. To convert low-quality food such as grass into body-building energy, an animal's digestive system has to break down tough cellulose fiber. One group of animals, which includes cattle, deer and sheep, do this by ruminating—they eat then later regurgitate the food, and chew it again slowly to draw as much goodness out of it as possible. Horses have a less efficient digestive system and have to spend more time eating than other grazers.

▲ RIVER HORSE

Hippopotamuses graze for a few hours each night, delicately plucking grasses with their broad, horny lips. Although they are huge animals, they can manage on about 90 pounds of grass each night because they rest in the water all day.

▶ HIGH LIVING

In Africa's open woodland savanna, giraffes browse the tops of trees that are out of reach to other herbivores. Their prehensile (grasping) lips and long, flexible tongues can pick out the most digestible and tasty leaves. Giraffes eat in the cool parts of the day and chew the cud while resting in the hot midday.

▲ TINY PUDU

The pudu of South America is the world's smallest deer. It lives in beech forests, feeding on flowers, fruit, bark and other vegetation. Like other deer and cattle, it spends a lot of its time resting and chewing the cud.

▲ TRAVELLING COMPANIONS

The wildebeest, or gnu, are grazers of the African plains. Every dry season, when their food supply is exhausted, these big antelopes move to fresh pastures with permanent water and shade. They travel in vast herds along well-worn routes, joined by zebra and other grazing animals.

▲ VARIED DIET

Warthogs feed almost entirely on grasses. After the rains, they pluck the growing tips with their incisor teeth or their lips. At the end of the rains they eat grass seeds, and in the dry season they use the hard upper edge of their nose to dig up roots.

▼ HIGH-SPEED GAZELLE

Thomson's gazelles use the same food-plants as other grazers of the African plains, but each animal eats a different part of the plant. Zebras tackle the tough woody bits, wildebeest eat the leaves, and gazelles nibble at the new growth beneath.

▼ FIGHTING HORNS

Male bighorn sheep, like other ruminants, make use of their horns when defending their territory or their females. Bighorn sheep have adapted to a wide range of habitats in North America, from desert to chilly alpine areas. They establish seasonal pathways to fresh grazing grounds when food runs out in the harsh winters. As they bound over rocky ground, their padded feet grip and absorb the shock of impact.

Horse Power

Cows and other ruminants have an extra chance to chew every bit of goodness from their vegetable diet. Horses, however, have to gain their nutrients by eating more, but are able to survive and thrive on grass, the most nutrient-poor diet of all.

The horse's digestive system processes large quantities of food in order to extract enough energy. They have an extra-long digestive system—of around 100 miles—to push as much food as they can through their bodies and convert it quickly to energy. Horses run on a virtually nonstop cycle of eating, digesting and producing waste. In the wild, they graze for about 16 hours a day, from early in the morning until around midnight. Horses can survive on poor vegetation as long as there is plenty of it. Cattle can manage with less food, as long as it is of a reasonable quality.

▲ CHEWING STYLE

A horse's slow, deliberate style of eating ensures that food is thoroughly ground down. Horses nibble vegetation with their front incisor teeth, then grind it down with their molars before swallowing. They chew slowly and wash the food down with plenty of saliva to aid digestion.

◀ HARD TIMES

Cold weather has made the ground hard, and snow covers the scant winter vegetation. These horses must paw at the ground to uncover the grass and dig up roots. They may even eat tree bark. Weak horses may not survive a hard winter.

STRESS IN THE STABLE ▶

When domestic horses are brought into stables they are fed well but often only three times a day. This is very different from a horse's natural feeding pattern, which is continuous and varied grazing. Bored stabled horses sometimes develop "vices," such as crib-chewing, tongue swallowing and rug-chewing. Although a domesticated horse may be given nutritious fodder, it is starved of its natural behavior.

◀ SURVIVAL IN DRY LAND

Grevy's zebras live in dry thornbush country on the African plains. If water is scarce, they migrate to the highlands. They can survive, however, on grasses, or even bushes, that are too tough for other herbivores to eat. They also dig waterholes—and defend them fiercely.

▲ WATERHOLE

Wild horses drink daily, although they can go without water for long periods of time. Most animals only drink fresh water. Wild asses and some species of zebra can tolerate brackish (stale, salty) water. This gives them a better chance of surviving droughts than fellow grazers, such as antelope.

▲ ALTERNATIVE FOODS

A horse from the New Forest, England, uses its flexible lips to pick some gorse flowers. Horses often choose more interesting foods than grass when they are available. They push out unwanted bits with their tongue.

Elephant Appetites

As herbivores, elephants only eat plants. Their diet is much more varied than that of horses, however, as it is made up of more than 100 different kinds of plants. Elephants eat leaves, flowers, fruit, seeds, roots, bark and even thorns, but still need huge quantities to gain enough nutrients to survive. They spend about 16 hours a day picking and eating their food. As with cattle and horses, millions of microscopic organisms live inside an elephant's gut, which help it to digest food. Even with the help of these organisms, half the food eaten by an elephant is not digested when it leaves the body.

▲ STRIPPING BARK
An elephant munches on tree bark, which provides it with essential minerals and fibre. The elephant pushes its tusks under the bark to pull it away from the tree trunk. Then it peels off a strip by pulling with its trunk.

◄ EATING THORNS
Elephants do not mind swallowing a mouthful of thorns – as long as there are some tasty leaves attached. Leaves and thorns are an important part of an elephant's diet as they stay green in the dry season long after the grasses have dried up. This is because trees and bushes have long roots to reach water deep underground.

▼ GRASSY DIET
Marshes are packed full of juicy grasses. About 30–60 per cent of an elephant's diet is grass. On dry land, an elephant may beat grass against its leg to remove the soil before feeding.

BABY FOOD ►

Young elephants often
feed on the dung of
adult elephants. They
do this to pick up
microscopic organisms
that will live inside their
gut and help them
digest food. Youngsters
learn what is good to
eat by copying their
mothers and other
adults. They are also
curious and like to
try new types of food.

◄ DUNG FOOD

Elephant dung provides a feast for dung
beetles and thousands of other insects.
They lay their eggs in the dung, and the
young feed on it when they hatch. Certain
seeds only sprout in dung after having first
passed through an elephant.

EATING IN CAPTIVITY ►

Meals for captive elephants include grasses and
molasses (a type of sugar). Zoo elephants eat hay,
bread, nuts, fruit, leaves, bark and vegetables.
They need huge amounts. In the wild,
elephants eat 225–450 pounds of plants every
day—that equates to about 1–2,000 carrots!

Food in Season

Although bears are classified as meat-eating animals (carnivores), most of them eat whatever is available at different times of the year. They have binges and put on fat in times of plenty, then fast when food is scarce. Brown (grizzly) bears are typical of most bears in that they eat an enormous variety of food, from grasses, herbs and berries to ants and other insects. They also catch salmon, rodents and birds, and on rare occasions hunt bigger game, such as caribou and seals. Only polar bears eat almost entirely meat—usually young seals. In summer, however, they supplement their diet with grasses and berries. All bears, even bamboo-loving pandas, scavenge on the carcasses of prey left by other animals. To track down their food, bears rely mainly on their keen sense of smell. Their snouts are well-developed in relation to their small ears and eyes.

▶ **HUNTING DOWN A MEAL**

This American black bear has caught a white-tailed deer fawn. Both black and brown bears are successful hunters. They are able to ambush large animals and kill them by using their considerable bulk, strong paws and jaws. The size of the bear determines the size of its prey. Large brown bears may prey on moose, caribou, bison, musk ox, seals and stranded whales. The smaller black bears take smaller prey, such as deer fawns, lemmings and hares. Roots, fruit, seeds and nuts, however, form up to 80 percent of the diet of both species.

Goldilocks
Bears are often featured in children's stories, such as Goldilocks and the three bears. They are regularly portrayed as friendly animals. However, bears are not always so friendly, they plot to ambush their prey and use their size to overcome them.

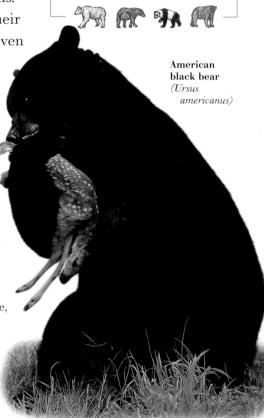

American black bear
(*Ursus americanus*)

WALRUS CITY ▶

Polar bears arrive on the northern coast of Russia each summer to hunt walruses that have gone there to breed. Enormous adult walruses shrug off attacks, but the young walrus pups are more vulnerable.

▲ BEACHCOMBING

Brown bears visit rivers and estuaries, hoping for a fishy meal. They overturn stones to find crabs and crayfish underneath. Bears are also attracted to rubbish on beaches and campsites.

▲ INSECT EATERS

Two sloth bear cubs from southern Asia learn to dig up termites. Sloth bears use their sickle-shaped claws to break open ant hills, bees' nests and termite mounds. They have developed an ingenious way of collecting their insect food. First they blow away any dust. Then they form a suction tube with mouth and tongue, through which they vacuum up their food.

▲ FRUIT LOVERS

An American black bear snacks on the ripe berries of a mountain ash tree. It carefully uses its incisors (front teeth) to strip the berries from their woody stem.

39

Fishing Match

Brown and black bears sometimes overcome their reluctance to be with other bears when there is plenty of food available. This often happens on the rivers of the northwest coast of North America. Thousands of salmon come in from the sea and head upriver to spawn (lay their eggs). The bears fish alongside each other at sites such as rapids where the water is shallower and the salmon are easier to see. An uneasy truce exists between the bears, although isolated fights do occur. The salmon runs take place at different times of the year, but the most important are those in the months leading up to winter. The bears catch the oil-rich salmon to get the extra fat they need to see them through the long winter ahead.

▲ **STRIPPED TO THE BONE**
Having caught a fish, the bear holds it firmly in its forepaws. Then it strips the skin and flesh from the bones.

◄ **EASY MEAL**
Salmon sometimes jump right into a bear's mouth. The bear stands at the edge of a small waterfall. Here the salmon must leap clear of the water to continue their journey upriver. All the bear needs to do is open its mouth.

40

◄ FIGHT FOR SPACE

Sometimes the uncertain truce between bears breaks down and they fight for the best fishing sites in the river. Young bears playfight, but older ones fight for real. An open mouth, showing the long canine teeth, is a warning to an opponent. If the intruder fails to back down it is attacked. Fights are often soon over, because the bears are keen to return to their abundant source of fish.

▲ FISHING LESSON

Bear cubs watch closely as their mother catches a salmon. The cubs learn by example and will eventually try it themselves. It will be a long time before they are as skilful as their mother.

▲ A SLOUTHE OF BEERYS

A group of bears is called a sloth. Brown bears on a salmon river are 'a sloth of grizzlies'. The term 'a slouthe of beerys' was used in the Middle Ages. It came from the word 'sloth' (laziness) as people thought bears were slow and lazy.

41

Wild Cat Feasts

All big cats are carnivores (meat-eaters). In the wild, they hunt and kill their own food and also steal kills from other animals. Cheetahs, however, only eat animals they have killed themselves. They patrol their neighborhoods, stalking prey. Other cats, such as jaguars, hide in wait before ambushing their victims. Many cats, including leopards, employ both tactics. In either case, camouflage is vital. Many of their prey can outpace them over distances, so big cats have to creep close to their victims unnoticed before going in for the kill.

King Solomon
Solomon ruled Israel in the 900s BC and was reputed to be very wise. His throne was carved with lions because of his admiration for these big cats who killed only out of necessity. In law, if a missing person was said to have fallen into a lion's den, it meant that there was no proof of his or her death.

◄ THE MAIN COURSE
A lion can kill large, powerful animals such as buffalo. A big cat usually attacks from behind or from the side. The prey may be too big to kill right away. If so, the cat knocks it off balance, takes a grip and bites into its neck.

CHOOSING A MEAL ►
A herd of grazing antelope and zebra keeps watch on a lioness crouched in the grass. The lioness lies as close to the ground as possible, waiting to pounce. When she has focused on a victim, she draws back her hind legs and springs forward.

42

▲ WARTHOG SPECIAL

Four cheetahs surround an injured warthog. The mother cheetah is teaching her three cubs hunting techniques. The cheetah on the right is trying a left paw side swipe, while another uses its claws. Cheetahs love to eat warthogs but also catch antelope and smaller animals such as hares.

▲ CAT AND MOUSE

A recently killed capybara (a large rodent) makes a tasty meal for a jaguar. Jaguars often catch prey such as fish and turtles in water. On land they hunt armadillos, deer, opossums, skunks, snakes, squirrels, tortoises and monkeys.

Did you know? Cheetahs will only chase prey if it runs. If it stops, so does the cheetah.

SLOW FOOD ▶

If a lion has not been able to hunt successfully for a while, it will eat small creatures such as this tortoise. Lions usually hunt big animals such as antelope, wildebeest, warthogs, buffalo, bush pigs and baboons. They work together in a group to hunt large prey.

Cats Go In for the Kill

Did you know? Lions try to flip porcupines onto their backs to avoid the sharp spines.

The way a wild cat kills its prey depends on the size of both predator and prey. If the prey is small with a bite-sized neck, it is killed with a bite through the spinal cord. Alternatively, a cat can crush the back of a small skull in its powerful jaws. Large prey is gripped by the throat so that it suffocates.

Cats stalk silently, their acute senses of sight, smell and hearing on the alert. Their large ears pick up the slightest sounds and can be turned to pinpoint the source of the sound.

▼ PAST ITS BEST
When big cats get old or injured it is very difficult for them to hunt. They eventually die from starvation. This lion from the Kalahari Desert in South Africa is old and thin. It has been weakened by hunger.

◄ FAIR GAME
A warthog is a delicious meal for a cheetah. Because the cheetah is quite a light cat, it must first knock over warthog-sized prey. It then bites the windpipe so that the victim cannot breathe.

▲ A DEADLY EMBRACE
A lioness immobilizes a struggling wildebeest by biting its windpipe and suffocating it. Lions are very strong. A lion weighing 330–550 pounds can kill a buffalo more than twice its weight. Lions live in groups called prides and the females do most of the hunting.

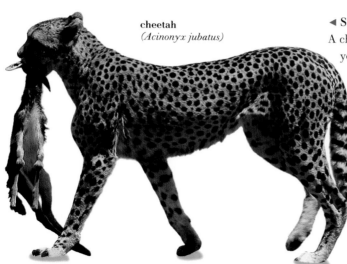

cheetah
(*Acinonyx jubatus*)

◄ SECRET STASH

A cheetah carrying off its prey, a young gazelle, to a safe place. Once it has killed, a cheetah will check the area to make sure it is secure before feeding. It drags the carcass to a covered spot in the bushes. Here it can eat its meal hidden from enemies. Cheetahs are often driven off and robbed of their kills by hyenas and jackals or even other big cats.

A SOLID MEAL ►

These cheetahs will devour as much of this antelope as they can. Big cats lie on the ground and hold their food with their forepaws when they eat. When they have satisfied their hunger, cheetahs cover up or hide the carcass with grass, leaves or whatever is available in order to save it for later.

► LIONS' FEAST

A pride of lions gathers around its kill. Lions often combine forces to kill large prey. One lion grabs the prey's throat, while the others attack from behind. The cats eat quickly before scavengers move in. Each has to wait its turn to eat. The dominant male usually eats first.

45

High-speed Cats

A cheetah is the world's fastest land animal. It can run at 70 miles per hour—the equivalent of a car being driven at high speed—but only over short distances. The cheetah's body is fine-tuned for short bursts of speed, with wide nostrils to breathe in as much oxygen as possible and specially adapted paws. Today, most cheetahs are found in east and southern Africa, with small populations in Iran and Pakistan. They live in many different kinds of habitats, from open grassland to thick bush, or even near-desert environments.

1 A pair of cheetahs creep up stealthily on a herd of antelope. Cheetahs hunt their prey by slinking slowly towards it, holding their heads low. They are not pouncing killers, like other big cats. Instead, they pull down their prey after a very fast chase. In order to waste as little energy as possible, cheetahs plan their attack first. They pick out their target before starting the chase.

2 The cheetah begins its chase as the herd of antelope starts to move. It can accelerate from walking pace to around 45 miles per hour in two seconds. Cheetahs have retractable claws (they can draw them in). However, unlike the claws of other cats, they have no protective sheaths. When drawn in, the exposed claws act like the spikes on the bottom of track shoes. This, combined with ridges on the paw pads, help cheetahs to grip when running.

3 At top speed a cheetah makes full use of its flexible spine and lean, supple physique. Its legs are very long and slender compared to its body. The cat can cover several metres in a single bound.

of the Plains

4 As the cheetah closes in on the herd, the antelope spring in all directions. The big cat changes direction at full speed. If it does not catch its prey within about 500 yards, it has to give up, as it can only keep up speed over short distances. Cheetahs usually hunt in the morning or late in the afternoon, when it is not too hot. Their life expectancy is short because their speed and hunting ability decline with age.

5 The cheetah may have to make several sharp turns as it closes in on its prey. Its long tail gives it excellent balance as it turns. The cheetah knocks its victim off balance with a swipe of a front paw. Most chases last no more than about 30 seconds.

6 Once the prey animal is down, the cheetah grabs the victim's throat. A sharp bite suffocates the antelope. Cheetahs are not strong enough to kill by biting through the spinal cord in the prey's neck like other big cats. They just hang on to the victim's throat until the animal is dead.

Hungry Canines

Wolves and other wild dogs are carnivores. They kill prey for fresh meat, but also eat carrion (dead animals). When no meat is available, they will eat fruit and berries, and also grass to aid digestion. As good long-distance runners, wild dogs can range over large territories in search of food. Packs of wolves target large herd animals such as moose, deer and caribou. They swim well and chase fish, frogs and crabs, but still spend much of their lives with empty bellies. When food is scarce, they sometimes rifle through rubbish near human settlements, or kill domestic animals such as sheep and cattle.

Most wild dogs have long, fanglike canine teeth to stab or pierce their prey. At the back of the mouth they have sharp-edged teeth for slicing through the flesh.

▲ NOT-SO-FUSSY FEEDERS
Raccoon dogs of eastern Asia eat all kinds of different foods, including rodents, fruit and acorns. Raccoon dogs also catch fish, frogs and water beetles and scavenge carrion and scraps from people's rubbish tips.

▼ CAUGHT BY COYOTES
Three coyotes tear at the carcass of a moose. These North American dogs usually hunt small prey such as mice. Sometimes they band together to go after larger creatures, or to gang up on other predators and steal their kills.

◄ FAST FOOD
A pack of dholes (an Asian species of wild dog) makes quick work of a deer carcass. Each dog eats fast to get its share—it may eat up to 9 pounds of meat in an hour. Dholes mainly eat mammals, but if meat is scarce they will also eat berries, lizards and insects.

▲ LONE HUNTER
A maned wolf is searching for food. Without a pack to help it hunt, this South American wolf looks for easy prey in open country, including armadillos and small rodents. It also eats birds, reptiles, insects, fruit and sugar cane.

▲ BEACH SQUABBLE
Two black-backed jackals squabble over the carcass of a seal pup. Jackals eat almost anything—fruit, frogs, reptiles and a wide range of mammals, from gazelles to mice. Jackals also scavenge kills from other hunters.

HIDDEN TREASURE ►
A wolf looks for a suitable spot in the snow to bury a freshly caught hare. After a pack has killed a large beast, or when a lone hunter has eaten its fill, it hides the remains of its food. Then, when food is scarce, the wolf can return to the hidden cache and retrieve its kill.

Did you know? All canids are quick feeders, but dholes in particular consume their food at a great rate.

grey wolf
(Canis lupus)

Wild Dog Hunt

The smaller species of wild dog, such as foxes and jackals, tend to hunt small prey, such as rodents, alone or in pairs. Some, including the solitary maned wolf, the bush dogs of the Americas and raccoon dogs, are mainly nocturnal (active at night). They rely on smell and hearing to find prey.

Dholes and African hunting dogs hunt in packs by day. They track prey by sight, smell and sound. Wolves hunt at any time of day or night. Hunting in packs means that larger prey can be tackled—ideally large enough to feed the whole pack. The size of a pack depends on the amount of food available in the area. Members of a pack work together like a sports team, with individuals providing particular strengths. Some may be good trackers, while others are fast or powerful. A hunt may last for several hours, but many are unsuccessful.

Little Red Riding Hood
In the story of Little Red Riding Hood, *a cunning wolf eats Red Riding Hood's grandmother. The wolf then steals the old woman's clothes to prey on the little girl. Fortunately a wood cutter rescues Red Riding Hood in the nick of time. After he kills the wolf, the grandmother emerges alive from inside its stomach.*

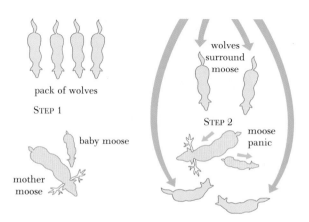

pack of wolves

STEP 1

mother moose

baby moose

wolves surround moose

STEP 2

moose panic

◄ **WOLF PACK IN ACTION**
Wolves use skill as well as strength to hunt large creatures such as moose. A calf is an easier target than an adult but will provide less meat. The wolves stalk their prey, then fan out and run ahead to surround the victim. Pack members dash forward to panic the animals and separate the mother from her baby. Once the young calf is alone, the wolves run it down and kill it by biting its neck.

DINGO KILL

Two dingoes have just caught a kangaroo. In the Australian outback, dingoes hunt a wide range of creatures, from tiny grasshoppers and lizards to large prey such as wild pigs and kangaroos. Sheep, introduced by settlers in the 1800s, are a favorite target.

◄ GROUP HUNTING

A large pack of wolves has killed a white-tailed deer. This amount of meat will not satisfy the group for long. Where food is scarce, a pack has to range over a much larger territory to find enough food. A pack will always hunt the largest game it can find.

coyote
(*Canis latrans*)

CLEVER TACTICS ►

A coyote plays with a mouse it has surprised in the snow. Coyotes often hunt mice. They leap high in the air to pounce on their victims. Coyotes have a more varied diet than wolves, feeding on fruit, grass, berries and insects, as well as mammals such as rabbits, deer and rodents. They take to the water to catch fish and frogs, and also steal sheep and chickens—which makes them unpopular with farmers.

Did you know To be in peak condition, a wolf needs to eat 9 pounds of meat a day.

▲ TEAMWORK

Working as a team, dholes hunt large prey such as sambar (a type of deer). Dholes whistle to keep in touch with one another as they surround their prey. Teamwork also helps the pack to defend the kill from scavengers such as vultures.

Hunting Dogs of

African hunting dogs eat more meat than any other wild dog. One in every three of their hunts ends in a kill, which is a very high success rate. They live on the savanna (grassy plains) of central and southern Africa, which is also home to vast herds of grazing animals such as wildebeest, gazelle and other antelopes. The pack wanders freely over a huge area, looking for herd animals to prey on. They rely on sight to find their quarry, so they hunt during daylight hours or on bright moonlit nights. They hunt mainly at dusk or dawn, when the air is coolest, and rest in the shade during the hottest time of day.

1 A pack of African hunting dogs begins to run down its quarry, a powerful wildebeest. On the open plains of the Serengeti in East Africa, there is little cover that would enable the dogs to sneak up on their prey. The hunt is often a straightforward chase. The hunt may be lead by a junior dog at the start of the pursuit.

2 The dogs run along at an easy lope at first. They have tested out the wildebeest herd to find an easy target. They look for weak, injured, or young and inexperienced animals that will make suitable victims. This wildebeest is an older animal whose strength may be failing.

the African Plains

3 A hunting dog tries to seize the wildebeest's tail. Members of the pack with different strengths and skills take on particular roles during the hunt. The lead dogs are in excellent condition and strong. They dodge out of the way if the wildebeest turns to defend itself with its sharp hooves and horns. Fast runners spread out to surround the victim and cut off its escape.

4 As the wildebeest tires, two dogs grip its snout and tail, pinning it down. Hunting dogs can run at 50km/hour for quite a distance, but their prey is much quicker. While the lead dogs follow the fleeing animal's twists and turns, backmarkers take a more direct line to save their strength. The rear dogs take over the chase as the leaders tire.

5 More dogs arrive and the strongest move in for the kill. While some dogs hold their victim by the snout and flanks, others jump up to knock it off balance. The dogs attack their victim's sides and rump and soon the animal is bleeding freely. It begins to weaken through shock and loss of blood.

6 The wildebeest crashes to the ground and the dogs rip at its underparts to kill it There is little snapping and snarling as they eat, but the kill is fiercely defended if a scavenger such as a jackal comes close. Half-grown cubs feed first, then the carcass is ripped apart and bones, skin and all are eaten. Back at the den, meat is regurgitated to feed the cubs.

▲ HUNGRY GIBBON
Gibbons, from Southeast Asia, are mainly frugivores (fruit eaters) but they also eat leaves and occasionally insects and eggs. They are so light and have such long arms that they can hang from thin branches and pick the ripest fruit growing right at the ends.

► BANANA BONANZA
Orangutans live in the forest canopies of Southeast Asia. Fruit forms about 65 percent of their diet. The apes spread the seeds over a wide area by passing them in their droppings far from the parent tree. This female has found some bananas, but the football-sized fruit of the durian tree is another orangutan favorite. It contains a sweet-tasting but foul-smelling flesh, which they adore.

Forest Food for Apes

Apes live in the rainforests of Africa and Asia and feed on fruit and leaves. They also eat a small amount of animal food, such as insects. Chimpanzees have a more varied diet than other apes and occasionally eat red meat from birds and mammals, such as monkeys and young antelopes. Orangutans have also been seen eating young birds and squirrels.

Apes spend a lot of time traveling all over the forest to find their food. If they stayed in one place, they would quickly use up all the food. They remember the locations of the best fruit trees in their area, and know when they will bear fruit. Apes have to eat a lot because a diet that consists mainly of plant food is often low in nutrients. As they cannot digest the tough fibers (cellulose) in the stems and leaves, much of what they eat passes through their gut undigested.

▲ MASSIVE MEALS

Gorillas are mainly herbivores, munching their way through 20–30kg of greens (equal to 40 cabbages) every day. They smack their lips a lot and make other appreciative noises. Gorillas are careful eaters, often preparing their food by folding leaves into a roll, or peeling off inedible layers. They drop any unwanted stalks, in a neat pile.

▲ FOOD ALL AROUND

The upland rainforests of Central and eastern Africa are full of plant food for the mountain gorillas that live there. They eat leaves, roots and fruit, soft bark and fungi. The gorillas need to eat a lot of food, so meals last two to four hours at a time. They have big stomachs to store the food while it is being digested. Gorilla days are mainly spent walking and eating food, then resting between meals to digest it.

▲ RAIDING PARTY

Chimpanzees live in communities in West and Central Africa. They eat both meat and vegetable matter and may band together to form a raiding party to hunt small animals such as monkeys and bush pigs. A hunt may last up to two hours, involving high-speed chases and ambushes.

▼ CHIMP FEASTS

Chimpanzees spend about six hours a day feeding, mostly just after sunrise and just before sunset. They eat a lot of fruit, which makes up about 68 per cent of their diet, but they also eat leaves and other plant matter, as well as meat and insects.

chimpanzee
(Pan troglodytes)

55

Whale Feeding

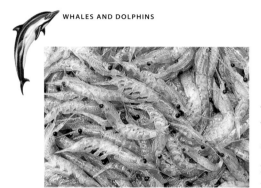

▲ CRUNCHY KRILL
These tiny shrimplike creatures known as krill form the diet of many baleen whales. Measuring up to 3 inches long, they swim in vast shoals, often covering areas of several square miles. Most krill are found in Antarctic waters.

About 90 percent of whales have pointed teeth that are ideal for grasping slippery fish. The other ten percent, known as baleen whales, do not have any teeth. Brush-like plates of horny baleen hang from the upper jaw. A baleen whale takes a mouthful of seawater and sieves it out through the baleen plates. Food, such as fish, algae and krill is held back in the baleen, and then swallowed. Toothed whales catch single fish, while baleen whales eat a mass at one time.

◀ PLOWING
A grey whale plows into the seabed, stirring up sand and ooze. It dislodges tiny crustaceans, called amphipods, and gulps them down. Grey whales feed mostly in summer in the Arctic before they migrate south.

southern right whale
(Euhalaena australis)

◀ SKIM FEEDING
With its mouth open, a southern right whale filters crustaceans, called copepods, out of the water with its baleen. The whale is huge, up to 80 tons, and it needs to eat up to two tons of the copepods daily. Usually, right whales feed alone, but if food is plentiful, several feed as they cruise side by side.

◄ SUCCULENT SQUID

Squid is the sperm whale's favorite food and is eaten by other toothed whales and dolphins as well. Squid are mollusks, in the same animal order as snails and octopuses. They have eight arms and two tentacles, and are called decapods (meaning ten feet). Squid sometimes swim together in dense shoals, of thousands.

Did you know? A blue whale eats nearly 2,250 pounds of krill in a single meal.

◄ TOOTHY SMILE

A Ganges river dolphin has more than 100 teeth. The front ones are very long. Ganges river dolphins eat mainly fish, and also take shrimps and crabs. They usually feed at night and find their prey by echolocation.

Ganges river dolphin
(Platanista gangetica)

► SUCKING UP A MEAL

Belugas feed on squid, small fish and crustaceans. Unlike common dolphins, belugas do not have many teeth. They suck prey into their mouths and then crush it with their teeth. Beaked whales also suck in their prey—mainly deep-sea squid—as their teeth are not suitable for grasping hold of fish.

▲ HUNT THE SQUID

The sperm whale is the largest toothed whale, notable for its huge head and tiny lower jaw. It hunts the giant squid that live in waters around 6,500 feet deep. At that depth, in total darkness, it hunts its prey by echo-location.

A Killer Whale

Among the toothed whales, the killer whale, or orca, is the master predator. It bites and tears its prey to pieces with its fearsome teeth and may also batter them with its powerful tail. It is the only whale to take warm-blooded prey. It may even attack a large baleen whale many times its size. As well as hunting seals, penguins, dolphins and porpoises a killer whale will also hunt fish and squid.Fortunately, there is no record of a killer whale ever attacking human beings. Killer whales live in family groups called pods. They often go hunting together, which greatly improves the chance of success.

1 A killer whale hunts by itself if it comes upon a likely victim, such as a lone sea lion. This hungry whale has spotted a sea lion splashing in the surf at the water's edge. With powerful strokes of its tail, it surges towards its prey. The whale's tall dorsal fin shows that it is a fullygrown male.

2 The sea lion seems totally unaware of what is happening but, in any case, it is nearly helpless in the shallow water. The belly of the killer whale is scraping the shore as it homes in for the kill.

on a Seal Hunt

3 Suddenly the killer's head bursts out of the water, and its jaws gape open. Vicious teeth, curving inward and backward, are exposed. It is ready to sink them into its sea lion prey. The killer whale has fewer teeth than most toothed whales, but they are large and very strong.

4 Now the killer snaps its jaws shut, clamping the sea lion in a vicelike grip. With its prey struggling helplessly, it slides back into deep water to eat its fill. Killer whales are in danger of stranding themselves on the beach when they lunge after prey. They usually manage to wriggle their way back into the sea with the help of the surf.

Sea Hunters

Most sharks are fearful carnivores and streamlined swimmers with an amazing sense of smell. Some make the most of their powerful, torpedo-shaped bodies to chase or pounce suddenly upon their prey. Others can be more leisurely, as they have special tracking and hunting adaptations. The lantern shark has organs on its skin that produce light and lure prey to certain death. The wide-spaced eyes of the hammerhead give it a wide field of vision to spot its favorite food, sting rays. The shortfin mako is one of the world's fastest sharks and can leap high above the water's surface. The white shark can leap, too, and has an awesome set of razor-sharp teeth to rip into large prey such as seals and dolphins.

▲ FEEDING FRENZY
Large quantities of food will excite grey reef sharks, sending them into a feeding frenzy. If divers hand out food, the sharks will circle with interest, until one darts forward for the first bite. Other sharks quickly follow, grabbing at the food until they seem out of control.

▲ FOREVER EATING
A large shoal of mating squid provides a great feast for blue sharks. The sharks feed until full, then empty their stomachs to start again!

▲ FISH BALL
A group of sharks can herd shoals of fish into a tight ball. The sharks will then pick off fish from the outside of the ball, one by one.

▶ NOT POWERFUL ENOUGH

The black-tipped shark is generally a powerful swimmer, but this one was caught by a larger relative, the bull shark. Black-tipped sharks hunt in the shallow waters of tropical seas, using their amazing sense of smell. Small fish hide out of reach in rocky crevices to escape.

Did you know? The great white shark sometimes eats crabs and lobsters.

◀ OCEAN DUSTBIN

Most sharks will eat anything that swims into their territory, and many are scavengers. Tiger sharks, though, are notorious for the variety of their diet. They have been known to eat coal, rubber tires, clothes— and humans— and they move into coastal waters at night to feed. They are found all over the world and grow to a length of 18 feet.

▼ BITESIZE CHUNKS

The cookie-cutter shark feeds by cutting chunks out of whales and dolphins, such as this spinner dolphin. The shark uses its mouth like a clamp, attaching itself to its victim. It then bites with its razor-sharp teeth and swivels to twist off a circle of flesh.

spinner dolphin
(Stenella longirostris)

▲ OPPORTUNISTS

Sharks will often follow fishing boats, looking for a free meal. This silvertip shark is eating pieces of tuna fish that have been thrown overboard.

61

Glossary

ambush
To hide and wait, and then make a surprise attack.

arthropod
An animal without a backbone that has many jointed legs and an exoskeleton on the outside of its body. Arthropods include spiders, insects, crabs and pill bugs.

brackish
Water that is not fresh and is slightly salty.

browser
A plant-eating animal that feeds on bushes and trees.

burrow
A hole in the ground, usually dug by a small animal for shelter or defence.

camouflage
The colors or patterns on an animal's body that allow it to blend in with its surroundings.

carcass
The dead body of an animal.

carnivore
An animal that feeds on the flesh of other animals.

carrion
The remains of a dead animal.

crocodilian
A member of the group of animals that includes crocodiles, alligators, gharials and caimans.

cultivated
Land or soil that is especially prepared and used for growing crops.

diet
The range of food an animal eats.

digestion
The process by which food is broken down so that it can be absorbed into the body.

domestic
Animals that do not live in the wild but are kept as a pet or farm animal.

dragline
The line of silk on which a spider drops down, often to escape danger, and then climbs back up.

drought
A prolonged amount of time without any rainfall.

equids
Horses and horselike animals, such as asses and zebras.

grazer
An animal that feeds on grass, e.g. horses, antelopes.

herbivores
Animals that only eat plant food.

herd
A group of particular animals that remain together, such as elephants or wildebeest.

incisor-teeth
A sharp-edged tooth in the front of a mammal's mouth that is used for biting and nibbling food.

intestine
Part of an animal's gut where food is broken down and absorbed into the body.

krill
Tiny crustaceans that are the main food for many of the baleen whales.

Latin name
The scientific name for a species. An animal often has many different common names. For example, the bird called an osprey in Europe is sometimes referred to as a fish hawk in North America. The Latin name prevents confusion because it never alters.

mammal
A warm-blooded animal with a backbone. Most have hair or fur. Mammals breathe air and feed their offspring on milk from the mother's body. Whales and dolphins are mammals, although they live in the sea.

mandibles
The jaw-like mouthparts that are present in some insects.

mantling
The behavior of birds of prey in which they spread their wings to conceal a catch. This is to prevent other hungry birds from stealing their kill.

mobbing
When prey birds gang up against their predators and try to drive them away.

nectar
A sweet liquid found in flowers and drunk by insects.

nectary
A specialized gland in flowering plants that secretes nectar. This is usually situated at the base of the flower.

nocturnal
Animals that are active at night.

nutrients
Substances that provide essential nourishment.

palp
A jointed sense-organ attached in pairs to the mouthparts of insects.

parasites
Animals that live on other animals and harm them by feeding on them, although they do not usually kill them. Fleas and ticks are parasites.

pesticides
Chemicals that are sprayed on to plants to kill pests, especially insects.

photosynthesis
The process whereby green plants manufacture carbohydrates from carbon dioxide and water, using the light energy from the sun.

plains
An area of flat land without any hills.

predator
An animal that hunts and kills other animals for food.

prehensile
A part of an animal that is adapted for grasping, e.g a giraffe's lips.

prey
An animal that is hunted by other animals for food.

proboscis
The long, tongue-like mouthparts of certain insects, such as the butterfly, which act like drinking straws to suck up liquid.

raptor
Any bird of prey. From the Latin *rapere* meaning to seize, grasp or take by force.

regurgitate
To bring up food that has already been swallowed.

reptile
A scaly, cold-blooded animal with a backbone. This group includes tortoises, snakes and crocodilians.

ruminant
An even-toed, hoofed mammal, such as a cow, which eats and later regurgitates its food to eat again to extract as much nourishment as possible.

savanna
A large area of grassland in tropical and subtropical areas, particularly in Africa. Savannas may have scattered trees and bushes but there is not enough rain for forests to grow.

scavenger
An animal that feeds on the remains of dead animals.

stooping
When a falcon dives on its prey from height at great speed, with its wings nearly closed.

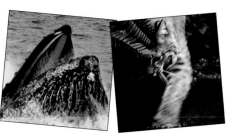

streamlined
To be shaped so as to move smoothly and efficiently with a minimum resistance to air or water. A shark's streamlined body enables it to move quickly through the water.

suffocation
To be killed by a lack of air because the air passages are blocked. A snake can coil its body around its prey to stop it from breathing.

talon
A hooked claw, especially on a bird of prey.

Index

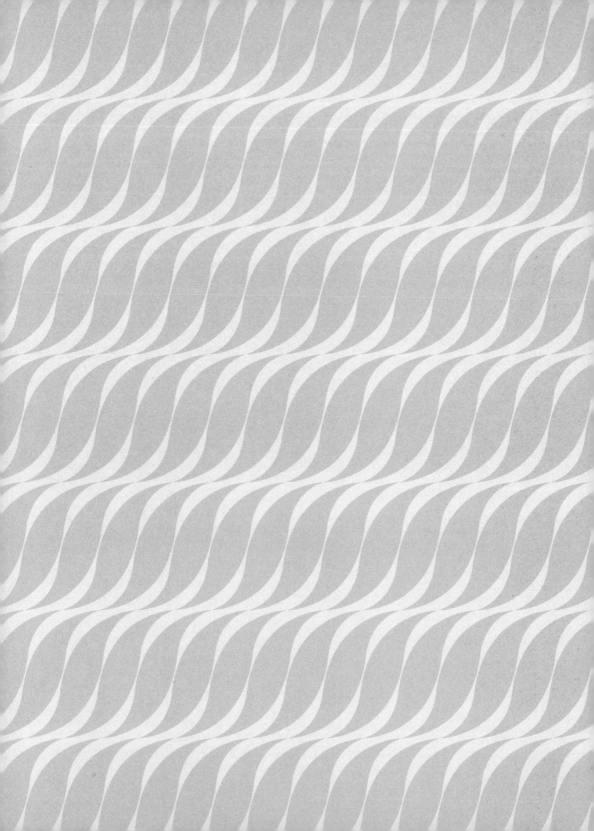